Spotlight Poets

Sunshine Through the Rain

Edited by Heather Killingray

Spotlight Poets

First published in Great Britain in 2004 by
SPOTLIGHT POETS
Remus House
Coltsfoot Drive
Peterborough
PE2 9JX
Telephone: 01733 898102
Fax: 01733 313524
Website: www.forwardpress.co.uk

SB ISBN 1 84077 125 9

Foreword

As a nation of poetry writers and lovers, many of us are still surprisingly reluctant to go out and actually buy the books we cherish so much. Often when searching out the work of newer and less known authors it becomes a near impossible mission to track down the sort of books you require. In an effort to break away from the endless clutter of seemingly unrelated poems from authors we know nothing or little about; Spotlight Poets has opened up a doorway to something quite special.

Sunshine Through the Rain is a collection of poems to be cherished forever; featuring the work of eleven captivating poets each with a selection of their very best work. Placing that alongside their own personal profile gives a complete feel for the way each author works, allowing for a clearer idea of the true feelings and reasoning behind the poems.

The poems and poets have been chosen and presented in a complementary anthology that offers a variety of ideals and ideas, capable of moving the heart, mind and soul of the reader.

Heather Killingray

Contents

The Authors
& Poems

Samantha Vaughan

I was born, Samantha Rhoda Lane now Vaughan, in a sunny town in South Africa where I lived for most of my life. Brought up in the summer sunshine, shunning the winter's cold. Yet when I met my future husband I hesitated not to move half way across the world to London just to be with him. Leaving behind my friends and family - but I have now a beautiful family of my own.

I have been writing poetry since I was 11 years old - which started off as just a release now and again for my emotions. As the years have passed my poetry writing has become my full time hobby. Inspiration seems to strike at any time, even waking me in the middle of the night with a poem running through my head.

Writing poetry for me now: I enjoy making cards and gifts for my friends and family where I can write a poem especially personalised just for them. Inspiration comes in many forms for me - more often than not I write about how I am feeling, the day to day goings on around me, my children are a big inspiration to me. They are so animated in what they do and say it brings such natural words that spring to mind to describe them.

With my words I try to paint a picture for the reader of how I see something. When I write about people I write about how I see them, their actions, and their moods. How our friendship has developed or how much the relationship/person means to me.

Poetry is part of my soul, words that bring me release to express feelings, say things that I am unable to speak. Enabling me to bring a little bit of joy to those around me.

Farewell I Say

For farewell I say
to thee that I love
falling behind the dark curtains
of depression that
closes round mine heart
eroding the happy
sunshine that once
shines through my smile
and brightened my life
of friends that have slipped
by the wayside not caring
or believing
how truly sad the
darkened heart may be
farewell again
may I see you in Heaven.

Carol

The beauty of your heart
That shines through your guarded eyes
Tragedy that guards your smile
Weariness of people unknown
Fear of affection of giving your heart
Terror of rejection, boldness, strengths
Running through you; take life as it offers
To make the most of what there is
To be loved, nurtured
Hold in your hand the precious ones
Few that have passage to your heart
The real you? Has anyone met the real you
Not the person portrayed
Before the walls that keep you safe
Ever watchful eyes, watching listening
Even at arms length just learning
Tragedy of age built the walls
Can love, friendship of arms length
Ever penetrate, to mean something dear.

Dianity

Dynamite of giggling energy
That springs from your soul
Laughter that dances in your eyes
Naughtiness yet rebellion
Of harsh rules, that need to be broken
Fun that bubbles through causing smiles to erupt
Form the saddest of souls, tears that spring
Forth - quickly dried by the
Formulation/beginning of a new adventure
Stubbornness that streaks
Through, to the point of distraction
Yet the boundaries are safety set
Not for the punishment as thought
Yet giggly girl, my friend
Your heart of the purest kind
Willingness to help, talk to laugh
That will stand you in good stead for the day
That brings the equal of your heart
That will radiate the sunshine from your soul
When happiness travels through your veins.

Shattered Dreams

Shattered dreams
Guarded emotions
Flying amongst the clouds
Hopeless realisations

Tears that are falling
Hidden sunshine
Echoed in your name I'm calling
Long beneath the sheltered mountains.

The Love You Both Share

Love is of unspoken moments
Circling your soul
Winged lightness when your heart takes flight
Glowing feelings that sends
Sparkling shivers dancing
In your eyes
Electric passion that passes
Not through your touch
But the tender tones
Whispered in daily chatter
Special spontaneous moments
That mean as much as the classic
Hug or those three words
That melt the heart
Love that you
Two undoubtedly share.

Winter's Gasp

Howling wind, spattering snow
Winter's fingers of coldness have
Gently tiptoed into our world
Fading out the warm summer sunshine
Replacing it with the cold sharps of
A winter's wind, that cause us to gasp
As we step from the warmth into the arms
Of cold winter winds - bringing days of
Sparkling darkness, with howling winds against
The velvet sky.

Nature's Beautiful Day

Flowers so beautiful
Have you ever noticed
The blanket of colour
Like a Mexican wave
Covers the land
Moving gently as the wind
Whispers through the petals
Daffodils trumpeting a melody
To the rising sun
The dandelions keeping time
To the beating rays
Daisies spiralling like windmills
Casting colours all around
The flower of love swaying
So gently to the dandelions' melody
The velvet petals of the rose soaking up the sun.

Farewell My Child

I cry for you my child
For I shall never see
Your eyes smiling up at me
Never feel your fingers
Tightly wound round mine
Never hear your gurgles,
Your laughter, your speech
You have gone back to be an
Angel my love
I must say my goodbyes
My heart is heavy
My tears aplenty
Come and visit me from time to time
Until then my little one
I whisper my goodbyes in the wind
And pray that the stars
Shoot my message to you
God bless, rest in peace.

A Stutter On My Tongue

Words seem to stutter on my tongue
as my mind races ahead
how unsure I am that what
I need to say will come out right
but as my pen hits the paper
the words seem to flow continuously
as if plugged into my mind
I know that my hand and my heart
are connected
my message seems okay
verses of words
calming instead of anger
how grateful I am
for the gift that helps me
to overcome the stutter
of the words on my tongue.

A New Day

Have you ever heard
The beautiful song of the
Birds as they greet the morning
As fingers of sunshine
Begin to reach across the land
Catching the dewdrops
Dangling off the spider webs
The colour seems to brighten the day
Flowers swaying gently
In the breeze
The grass as soft as velvet
Beneath your bare toes
The beauty of morning
Brings but a smile to our face
The sweet melody of the birds
Rings harmony to our ears
A beautiful way to start a morning.

A Simple Smile

I am sending a smile
To the depths of your soul
Warming your heart
Tingling in your eyes
To bring happy thoughts
To a cloudy day
Washed away by the
Warmth of the knowledge
That a friend truly cares
To express the notion
Of love by a simple smile.

The Beauty Of Raindrops

The pure melody of the rolling thunder
That settles in the clouds
Sending across the sky's rays
Of sparkling lightning
That brings brightness to the darkness
Illuminating the back drop
Of velvet sparkles with streaks of beauty
Settling peace within you
As the gentle rain begins to fall.

Dancing Rainbows

Silent raindrops that fall,
Beating in time to the howling wind
That spatters gently across the window
All the while rainbows
Dance in the pearl drops
That dangle from the trees
Elegance of silent teardrops
That fall from the fluffy clouds
Beating on the heat of the ground
Sending only warmth of beauty that shines forever.

On The Wings Of Angels

On the wings of angels
Sent with love
Curled in teardrops
Filled with laughter
Surrounding the pain
The joy of friendship
Times filled with
Crystal drops
Falling like waterfalls
Yet the happiness
Of joy dear friend brings
Fills the hope
Of an uncertain tomorrow
With a heart filled
With love
With friendship.

Callin

Dependability of a little soul
So young, innocent, free
Unlaboured by the restrictions
Of responsibility's naivety of the world
Yet the beauty of each cheeky grin
Naughty moment, soulful eyes of unconditional love
That passes into phases of unsurety
During life of adult and teenager
Yet the rainbow of days
Of discovery along your road of life
That starts with our guidance
Supported by our love brings challenges
Made easier by the bond of mother and child
That connects our souls as one stubborn individuality
Strength of unabounded measures
That will feed your fuel for conquering
Each challenge along your journey of life
Supported and loved now and forever by us.

Moments Of Memories

Moments of memories that
Trickle in your heart that erupt
The waterfall of tears as the
Grief surrounds your soul
Squeezing your heart back
Together slowly as time passes
Memories that one day will
Be remembered fondly, that
Will help ease the hurt into
The recess of your heart.

Tristram Uvedale Francis Barrington

Born 20th March 1915. Journalist. Married to Elizabeth Frances Eden-Pearson 8th September 1939. Lives in Weybridge, Surrey. One daughter.

Appointments: Morning Post; Assistant Editor, Aeropilot; Managing Editor, Hulton Publications 1960/61; Editorial Manager, Longacre Press, 1961/1962; Director of Information and Broadcasting, Basutoland, 1962-1967; Director of Information, UK Freedom from Hunger Campaign, 1967-1973; Founder Editor, World Hunger.

Publications: 'Adventure in Oil, 1958; John Fisher; Basutoland, 1961.

Contributions to: Sunday Telegraph; Time & Tide; Tablet; Universe; Catholic Herald; Commercial Times.

Honours: Rics Award, Best Property column in weekly paper, 1988, 1991; ISVA Provincial Property of the Year, 1990.

Memberships: Master of the Keys, Guild of Catholic Writers, 1987-1991, Deputy Master, 1991-1993, Institute of Journalists.

Poetry themes: Religion, relationships; nature.

Love's Vision

Oh we have touched the heart of love.
This is love and in loving,
Still do my lips kiss those sweet shadows
Where your memory is.
Cleopatra and her Antony,
Ronsard and young Romeo,
Heloise and Abelard -
We are their peers. With no great wonder
Did they upon their lovers' lips wreak plunder.
Our souls like their in beauty yielded then,
Never to be their own in loneliness again.
As sun brings flowers when winter's nearly done,
As moon draws gently on a tide that's just begun,
We could not then nor can discover now
What blessed vision touched us,
Nor how this love in which our lives
As jewels are set like calmest water
In a coin of the land inlet puts all earth,
All matchless beauty in our debt.

Broadwater Autumn

God has clothed these trees in autumn hues.
Some combine their summer green with gold
Some now greet the day in deepest red.
Cold winds move the silent lake and change
The algae carpet to clear unsullied stream
Sun and clouds reflected there.

The earth is spread with fallen leaves,
Green grass joined with myriad shades
And on the lake, the wild birds glide,
Heron, swans with coot and hern,
Changing now to swift and sudden flight
While hungry pike make daring leaps.

God has moved the lake with gentle breeze
And blessed the water with His grace
Where sunbeams dance upon the stream
And autumn trees are mirrored there
With sun and cloud at water's edge,
Sign and pledge of God's beauty and His love.

Vanished Muse

Where has the vanished wonder gone
That filled my heart each day?
No more do visions fall
Where the morning glory shone
Upon the new transcendent day
But still does secret beauty keep
Her troth with all my broken sleep.

O still the splendours of the sky remain
And fill the world each night
And still does earth resound
With nature's glad refrain
To greet the morning light
Where the fount of grace is found
In the world that God has made
And His miracles never fade.

Married Love

When I think of love in marriage blest
Through all the years of union and delight,
I thank my God for all that He has given,
For every new discovery and hours of calm and rest,
All the times of darkness, all the times of light,
In our harmony of minds, by love and beauty driven.

Together or apart, our lives in love remained.
In peace and ear, our minds together stayed,
God's gift to us for more than sixty years.
Through the flight of time, all friction was disdained,
In the blessed hours when life and laughter played
And in times of stress and sudden fear.

Death came down to tear our lives apart
And send us on our separate ways,
But past the labyrinths of earth
New life will bend each soul and heart
Beyond the mists of parting days
And changed to joy the tears of dearth.

When I Pray

Eternal wisdom when I pray
Oh let me hear thy voice
That through the silence sounds
Oh lead me on thy way
And make my heart rejoice
When thy perfect love resounds.

Eternal Father when I pray
Let my words be thine
Taught me by thy son.
Thy will be done each day
In peace and light divine
In thy sight till day is done.

Holy Spirit when I pray
Send thy light within me.
Trinity of love and life
Take my heart each day;
Bind my soul to thee
Free at last from earthly strife.

Towards A Diamond Wedding
September 8 1939-September 8 1999

(For E F T)

Our love has spanned near sixty years,
In war and peace, in the good times and the bad.
Our vows with sacraments were sealed
And burgeoned through all our hopes and fears
In all our years apart, in the good days and the sad,
In the crises of our lives; in sudden stress concealed.

Our love was blessed with gifts of grace
In direst war, in the longed for end of strife,
In our days together and in our times apart.
In shell-torn hills, I found your face
Serene above the mists of life
And heard your voice within my heart.

We thank our God for all that He has brought
Within our lives, for the laughter and the tears,
For all the days of calm and all our peace at night.
We thank our God for all that He has taught
Through all the movement of the years,
For our enduring love and all its swift delight.

The Music Of The Earth

Can you hear the music of the earth
And feel all creation's joy?
God's love resounding every hour,
His glory in the rising of the sun,
His mercy in the fading of the light.
God's music echoes in the hills
And in the valley gently falls,
In the ocean plays upon the waves
And ever makes the river's song,
Meets the heartbeat of the praying man,
Joins the trembling of the maiden's voice,
Lifts the singing of the little child,
Takes the measure of the passing years,
Fills with hope all mankind.

Nightmare

I woke to find a lonely star
That shone upon a barren hill
Where strange in dark and light
There danced from near and far
The spectre of a weakened will
That sank beyond my sight.
It crouched upon the ground
And hid its deep scars there.
Three times I heard it sound:
'I fear; I fear; I fear.'
It made the darkness touch me
And stood in silence near me.
When I pleaded 'Change my heart,'
It stirred the crumbled dust
That lay beneath its feet
And muttered with a sudden start:
'Dead lust, dead lust,
No living soul is here for you to meet.'
Then from the caverns of the night
Beyond the falling precipice of pain,
Came the creatures of the deep
And grey phantoms in their flight
Above the ancient castles of the plain
And troubled all my sleep.

Penitence

May God forgive my wayward mind,
That leads my thoughts astray.
May God forgive each careless word I speak
And all the pain that others find
In my silence and in my words this day
Dear Lord forgive me when I cloud the joy that others seek.

May God forgive my sins of sight
And guide my eye to see His will
Within His word and sacrament.
Dear God forgive me when I spurn Thy light,
For all my faults be with me still,
Let me with Thy mercy be content.

Christ shape my sinful hands to pray
And lead my feet to follow Thee
Lord keep me always in Thy sight
At every step along the way
That leads at last to Calvary,
To resurrection and Thy redeeming light.

Alone

I am alone, yet not alone
Christ is beside me
Calming all strife
Flesh of my flesh, bone of my bone.
God is within me,
The Father of life.

I am alone, but not alone,
God's spirit within me
By day and by night.
I am alone, but not alone,
His presence around me
In wonder and light.

One in three and three in one
Eternal God of love and light,
I am alone, but not alone,
Thou art beside me, Thy will be done.
I pray within Thy sight,
Oh still bereft but not alone.

Oatlands Broadwater

The bare branched trees are etched against the winter sky,
Reflected on the sunlit lake
Where the gentle waters dance.
From the shadows bright birds fly
And swans spread wings for beauty's sake
While round the sun, the clouds advance

Beyond the lake by flooded pools
The horses graze on sodden grass.
While white gulls swoop and sway
In sudden spurts the duckling schools
Dive up and down and swiftly pass
The gliding swan on her majestic way

Beyond the lake, the river gleams
And sunlit meadows stretch to royal fields
Where the park of Windsor lies
Another lake serenely streams
And stillness now to whispered movement yields
Where air and water mingle sighs.

A Prayer For Faith

By thy birth in Mary's womb
Give me faith newborn each day.
By thy hidden childhood years,
By thy cross and empty tomb,
Give me strength to tread thy way
And shed my doubts and fears.

By thy fast of forty days
Unto penance bend my will,
By thy word and by thy life
Guide my heart in all thy ways,
Lead me to thy Holy Hill
Beyond the field of human strife.

By thy word and sacrament
Build my faith anew each day.
By thy prayer and desert fast,
By thy Eucharist and thy covenant
Give me light to see thy way
And reach thy kingdom at the last.

Winter

O can you hear the winter song
Now where the white gulls wheel and sweet
And wild the roe deer leap along?
O can you hear the cold earth sigh in sleep?

I can hear the whisper of the rain
Where the lake stream softly christens
The winter grass and trembles on again
To pools where sunlight faintly glistens.

I can see the waters gleam
Where the heron greets the dawn
And sunlight glides the stream
By the feet of the thirsty fawn.

And I can find a new delight
Upon the winter plain
And in the silence of the night
I can find new peace again.

God's Gifts

We thank thee Lord for thy gift of life and light
We thank thee for the wonder of creation;
We thank thee for the beauty of the earth
And all thy gifts of sound and sight.
We bless thee for our souls' elation
And for all thy help in time of dearth

Our lives are blessed with gifts of grace
In times of joy and in the midst of tears
In our hours of prayer, through thy hallowed name;
And I have wished to see thy face
To banish all my earthy fears
Redeemed at last from sin and shame.

We thank our God for all that He has brought
Within our lives, for the laughter and the tears
For all the days of calm and all our peace at night.
We thank our God for all that He has taught
Through all the passing of the years,
For His enduring love and its revealing light.

Down The Years 1915-2004

In thanking God I lift my grateful heart
For all His gifts of mercy and of care,
Childhood full of love and ever free from fear,
Cherished, guarded, kept from strife apart
And still of all God's beauty made aware.

When I think of love in marriage blest
Through all the years of union and delight,
I thank my God for all that He has given,
For every new discovery and time of calm and rest,
All the times of darkness, all the times of light
In our harmony of minds by love and beauty driven

Together or apart, our lives in love remained.
In peace and war, our minds together stayed,
God's gift to us through more than sixty years.
Through the flight of time, all friction we disdained,
In the happy hours when life and laughter played
And in the times of stress and sudden fear

Death came down to tear our lives apart
And send us on our separate ways
But past the labyrinths of earth,
New life will bind our soul and heart
Beyond the mists of parting days
And change to joy the tears of dearth.

Dorothy M Mitchell

I was born in a small Yorkshire village just before the second world war, hard times, air raid shelters, sky red with fire as enemy planes bombed nearby Bradford. My dad worked as a railway signalman, and part-time 'Dad's Army'. Mum cleaned at the local pub. Ration books and swapping coupons was a regular occurrence, 'make do and mend' was part of life then. Dad kept chickens, grew veg in the garden, we managed.

In 1953 we moved to Evesham. I was 16 years old, married at 18. First son arrived when I was 21. My second son at 27. I was diagnosed with multiple sclerosis in my late 30s. Suffered many relapses, I was widowed at 53. My life was at a low ebb, I met a friend who asked me to go to church with her. 'The Elim Pentecostal' in Evesham. Well, I couldn't feel any worse than I did, so off I went. That was to be the turning point in my life. This was what I needed, Pastor talked to me, I cried out my pain and asked Jesus into my life.

My present hubby attended the church. He was widowed a year before me. All at church were concerned for him, he was hurting so, I know Jesus sent me there so we could be together. Pastor married us 10 years ago, I was baptised on our first wedding anniversary.

3 years ago gentle poems started coming to me, Christian poems with a message, I feel the Lord is using me, I am humbled, blessed.

Hold On

I pray these words will touch a poor soul,
A dear one whose heart is breaking,
An angry word, a hasty tongue,
The wrong end of the stick has been taken.

I've been there, I know the score,
It's a nightmare in the making,
You can say so little to put things right,
Oh! the personal cross you are bearing.

The pain you are feeling deep inside,
Is nothing to do with bones aching,
You visit the doctor, he gives you pills,
That mask the hell that you're suffering.

The Lord knows your fears; He wipes all your tears,
He's crying with you, no question,
So try to hold on, this horror will pass,
Many find themselves in this situation.

Jesus won't let you down, He knows your pain,
You feel all that you are has been taken,
Rest in the arms of our Saviour, He cares,
Of His love, you won't be forsaken.

Forgive For Your Sake

Dearest Saviour, dearest Lord,
Come quiet me today,
Calm the tears, salve the hurt,
Poured o'er me yesterday.

The perpetrator of such anger
Hurled in such a way,
Surely needs to turn to Jesus,
On His knees to pray.

Our Lord turns from anger spoken,
He knows it's not the way,
His teaching is to show forgiveness,
To each other every day.

When you feel that old bad temper
Eating you away,
Forgive, forgive is Jesu's cry,
This is the only way,

Don't harbour hatred in your heart,
Let it go today,
Talk to Jesus, He will hold you,
And in His loving arms you'll stay.

Once Upon A Time

Once upon a time I was lost in sin,
Once upon a time I know,
Then I knew that joyous day how I needed Him,
Never would I let Him go,

Once upon the cross He died for me,
Once upon a time long ago,
All His pain and sorrow had to be,
Just because He loves me so,

Sorrow turned to joy,
In my Saviour's arms all because I love Him so,
My life to Him I give, as He gave His own,
Once upon the cross long ago.

A Country Lane

Just stroll along a country lane,
Upon a springtime morn,
Soft dewdrops glisten on the hedgerow,
Nature's drink at dawn,

Look around,
Breathe in the beauty now dark winter's gone,
Leave behind the cares of life,
That make you feel forlorn,

Surround yourself with nature balm,
Let go your personal storm,
Walk gently down that country lane,
Feel your spirits being reborn,

We each of us carry tears inside,
When our hearts and dreams are torn,
So wander on down that peaceful lane,
Find God's healing, and roses, not thorns.

I Do Try

Gazing out on my winter garden,
Wondering where to begin, to achieve,
The beauty my garden portrays,
I must start the work before spring,

Scrub the patio, mend the fence,
Bird boxes need a wash,
As do the planters, water features as well,
To neglect this would be my loss,

Clear up the debris, paint the gnomes,
They do love to look all posh!
Awaiting the wonder nature unfolds,
When dressed in her summer best,

But truth to tell with my limited knowledge,
In the garden I'm not the best,
Oh! thank goodness for hubby, who takes the strain,
I do a bit, he does the rest.

Gentle Arms

Gentle arms to hold me,
Loving eyes that see
All my deepest sorrow
No one else can see.

Tender heart you've won me,
Dried up all my tears,
Filled my life with sweet love,
Banished all my fears.

How I love You Jesus,
You're my world to me,
Loving Saviour hold me
For all eternity.

Our Feathered Friends

Our garden resembles a bird nursery restaurant,
With wet bread and butter the dish of the day,
Added to this fine grated best cheddar,
Crushed peanuts, washed down with Adam's pure ale.

The number of babies this year is alarming,
We are feeding non-stop, can't turn them away,
From five in the morning, till late in the evening,
Mums bring their chicks to our cafe to play.

As well as feeding, they are bathing with vigour,
Our patio is regularly washed with the spray,
It's a busy time for little birds' parents,
We give as much help as we can every day.

There is no charge for service provided,
We love them to come to our garden each day,
The pleasure we get is worth all the hard work,
God willing, our bird friends forever will stay.

Progress At A Price

Woodland and hedgerow, coppice and brook,
Birds' habitats vanishing now,
Demolished by man in his endless quest,
For new roads, new houses, new towns.

Many a lark, a ground dwelling bird,
Has lost her home for sure,
No more her song so sweetly sung,
Delivered on high in the air,

We seldom see the white throat,
The swallow or the swift,
They're all part of nature's store,
Our good Lord's precious gift,

Do we know the devastation
That progress often brings,
Have lost birds soared their way to Heaven,
Seeking home on heartbroken wing,

So take care of the birds that visit your garden,
Feed them, keep them strong,
Your reward will be great when summer arrives,
They will sing you their beautiful song.

Waiting

Winter casts her cold dark shadows,
Days shorten, nights so long,
Rain beats against the windowpane,
Howling winds so strong.

Fires blazing in the hearth,
The lights glow ever strong,
Warming food, a tasty stew,
The kettle for tea boiling on.

Second by second the days will grow long,
We will welcome another spring.
Bulbs will awaken from winter's sleep,
In rainbow multitudes, a throng.

A pale sun will shine to warm the ground,
Snowdrops and crocus arrive,
All dressed in their Sunday best,
Cold winter days all gone.

Birds will be nesting, morning chorus their joy,
Oh what a glorious sound,
Blackbird, and song thrush, on blossomed bow,
Will tell us winter is done.

More flowers will follow in radiant hue,
Our garden's complete 'ere long,
So patiently wait now for winter to pass,
For the best is yet to come.

By His Side

Once you open your heart to Jesus' love,
You won't be the same again,
When His care comes through you to others in need,
His love blossoms forth right then,

Let your lonely life find Him, answer His call,
He beckons with arms open wide,
Surrender to Jesus, He won't let you down,
He would love you to walk by His side,

He won't alarm you, He doesn't control,
Freely He gives you His love,
It comes from the Father, through Jesus to us,
Then back to our God above.

Never To Let Me Go

I was living my life, oh I was alright,
Isn't that how it should be,
Take care of yourself, number one rule,
Just look after me.

His spirit was calling but I knew Him not,
What could the Lord want of me?
A sinner who'd shunned Him, gone my own way,
In thought, uncaring, free.

But He knows me so well, the tears He could see,
I'd fallen so far, hurting so,
But He grabbed hold of me on Calvary's tree,
Never to let me go.

Oh the truth He could see, I needed Him so,
I was sorry as sorry could be,
Yes He grabbed hold of me on Calvary's tree,
Now I never will leave Him, oh no!

To The Cross For Me

You went to the cross Lord, and suffered for me,
You went to the cross Lord, and died for me,
You ascended to Heaven to Your Father above,
And showered the world with Your beautiful love,

You went to the cross Lord, and died for me,
You went to the cross Lord, on dark Calvary,
You ascended to Heaven to Your Father above,
And gave to the world Lord,
Your wonderful love,

You went to the cross Lord, my soul to save,
You went to the cross Lord,
Your life You gave,
Your Father was waiting with arms open wide,
And You went up to Heaven,
To reign by His side.

The Supreme Gardener

Our greenhouse is bursting with baby plants,
Protected from inclement weather,
The season is right, just turning late spring,
Entering early summer.

The garden is ready, cultivated and dug,
Given nutrients, and hoed with a fervour,
Added to this much patience and love,
Poured out in equal measure,

Flowers are planted in their home at last,
To delight us with radiant hue,
The bees and the birds will do all they can,
Cross pollinate colours new.

We can propagate, germinate,
Use all our skills, to eliminate every weed,
But we wouldn't have our gardens today,
If God hadn't first made the seed.

Cross Of Shame

You took my Lord, oh! cross of shame,
Struck with sword, He hung in pain,
Nails of sin pierced hands and feet,
A crown of thorns for Him so sweet,

And there He hung on Calvary's tree,
My precious Lord who died for me,
My sin He bore to set me free,
My heart I give in thanks to thee,

His father said come home my Son,
Your earthly work for Me is done,
Now in Heaven come take your place,
At my right hand,
In love and grace.

The Hill Of Golgotha

On the hill of Golgotha on Calvary's tree,
My Saviour died for me,
I didn't deserve the price that He paid as on the cross He died,
My sin He took the sacrifice made,
Oh Lord with me abide,

He cares so much, He died for us all, how could we ever forget,
It matters not if you're young or old,
We will meet Him in glory yet,

He reigns in Heaven with Father above,
Oh! what a victory,
He pours on the world His wonderful love,
Given for you and me,
On the hill of Golgotha on Calvary's tree,
My Saviour died for me.

Innocence

Oh! Holy baby meek and mild,
Born in a stable bare,
Sweet and humble, innocence sleeping,
Holy child so rare,

With the ox, the ass, and lamb,
Chosen to be there,
In the stable with sweet babe,
His joyous birth to share,

The angel of the Lord appeared,
Saying, Christ is born this night,
As shepherds in the fields were watching o'er
Their flocks, took fright,

In David's town is born of Mary,
The heavenly child so fair,
In a manger, in a stable,
You will find Him lying there,

Wise men journeyed from the east,
Guided by the star,
Bringing gifts for precious child,
Gold, frankincense and myrrh,

How the angels sang with joy,
With heavenly choirs on high,
The promised child this day is born,
That man no more may die,

Two thousand years or more have passed,
The story will ever stay,
Innocence born in a stable,
Of Mary, that first Christmas day.

Food For Thought

Holly and mistletoe, tinsel and fun,
Christmas trees, baubles and more,
Mother has baked the pies and cakes,
Is there enough, or should she bake more?

It's Christmas again,
The time of year when we buy presents galore,
A jumper for Dad,
Is it his size?
Will this perfume be right for Aunt Maude?

John wants a bike, Mary a doll,
Do its eyes open and close?
Is the fifteen pound turkey cooked tender or dry?
Buy good tights for Granny, fine hose,

The shops are all bursting with all we require
To make Yuletide go with a swing,
Carols are sung in melodious tone,
The bank balance looks a bit thin,

We will cope with card writing, overnight guests,
Almost all that the season entails,
But if two thousand years ago Jesus hadn't been born,
We wouldn't have Christmas today.

John Michael Cox

John Michael Cox, born 15 January 1923 in Cheshire. Early years were spent in hometown of Bristol, in a house overlooking Bristol Zoo.

Educated at Clifton College where my father was master. Many of my school holidays were spent with my grandfather in Saint Davids, Pembrokeshire with its wonderful cathedral and coastal countryside.

I served in the RAF 1942-46 w/o pilot in Canada, India and Burma. After the war I completed a degree in geology at Bristol University. Practised in England, Iraq and Alberta, Canada.

I have been in scientology since 1959 and on staff at the Hubbard College of Scientology for 29 years.

Interests include current affairs, history, getting at the truth of things, walking, and the countryside. In poetry the English poet Edward Thomas opened my eyes to the possibilities of blank verse and the Russian poets to the task of preserving values and human qualities in the midst of dire circumstances.

I like poetry for its compactness of language, for its imaging and for the possibility of expressing more than one level of meaning at a time, and for its kinship to song.

Christmas

Lord, You came two thousand years ago,
Walked the roads of Galilee,
Taught us in parables and story,
Gave us an example of how to live,
Showed us Your great kindness.
It is Your love
That has been at the heart
Of all that's best
In our northern land.
You are with those high or low
Who in trust try to follow You
And with those of other faiths
Who seek You under a different name.
Dear Lord - we were in darkness
And lost;
And You came.
Thank You!

Startide

Tattered leaves,
Drift in sidewalks,
And collect under trees.
Shoppers stream by,
Chattering, cheerful,
Some treasure laden,
As in an eastern caravan,
Where camels jingle softly along
And purple shadows
Play across the dunes;
Now subtle tinted,
With mauves, ochres and reds,
After days glare.

Whilst on the horizon,
Snow peaks,
Cold - lunar - serene,
Await the moon's green light.
So, once the Magi came,
From Persia;
Where they had gazed long hours
At complex patterns of stars and planets,
Sifted traditions, and interpretations,
Took counsel, calculated again.
Minds held and calmed,
As in some mandala.
Lifted for a moment above their times,
Good men, listening for the infinite whisper
Of a new thought and a new age.
Now single purposed, they travel westward,
Under the brilliant stars
To see where a great soul is born,
Their life's consummation and justification.
By tomorrow night they will have crossed
The Jordan,
Gone through Jericho's hot groves,
To reach the Judean uplands,
And frosty Bethlehem.
So we too, held by the busy scene,
May stand listening for the deeper meaning,
And sense what this new age may bring.
A hard frost stands poised,
Whilst the last yellow sunlight creeps
Up the steep walls,
Glints on metal roof cowlings
And is gone:
Save for the vapour trail
Of a homing airliner.
High! Brilliant! White!
Before the stars dance out.

Storm

Newgale, where the great seas roll in.
Giant white steps, one on top of the other,
Surge up to the pebble storm barrier;
In a sweeping rush of foam.
Gulls wheel against the bucketing air,
And are flung inland.
A tide line of wood,
Flotsam, old mine floats and seaweed
Clean washed, clean smelling,
And the gale buffets the watcher with spume,
Salt to the taste; bringing premature autumn
To the valley trees.
Overhead, grey clouds twist and turn
Racing eastwards,
Exulting in the unhindered wind.
And I conjuring this bright image
From boyhood years,
Think with gratitude,
Of my wonderfully kind mother
And gentle grandfather,
Playmate brother,
Together in a moment of time;
On that Pembrokeshire beach,
One January morning,
Before the war!

The Turn Of The Tide

Something strange happens
When the tide turns.
The surf has a different sound,
And the wind is not the same.
As when night is nearly over
But day not yet come;
Some declaratory boundary line
Has been crossed.
Barnacles and limpets heave a sigh
Of relief.
Abandoned pools come to life.
The whole long shore line
Takes on an expectancy,
It is as if myriad life forms
Are getting ready, stirring about.
Like passengers on a railway platform
When the distant signal drops,
Officials bustle around
People pick up their luggage,
Nervously put it down again
Sensing the unseen train's approach.
The whole atmosphere changes
When the tide turns.
And as the waters rise
Things are possible,
Which were not so before.

Hut Circles

(St David's Head)

Not wide. A man could lie
And touch wall to wall.
Perhaps seven or eight,
And on the seaward side,
A rampart of stones;
Still formidable after centuries' wear.
A little further inland
A lichened cromlech.
Stone table on two supports,
One gone, so tilted to a hollow triangle:
Chieftain's tomb of a warrior race.
Green cushions of thrift,
Bouncy, mixed with heather:
Sea upholstery
Of comfort rare,
On this wild headland.
But how would it be
When the great storms thundered in from the west?
Or the north east's insidious fingers
Felt for every unturfed hole;
Flung fire smoke
Every which way and that?
Or in sea mists cover
When wolves pushed closer in?
And the harper plucks expectant strings.
Cloaks fastened tight, all eyes eager turn.
Mood established with urgent chords,
The magnificent language weaves in and out
Of the heroic tale,
Modulates in passages of great tenderness
For far off princesses,
Rises to the ring of bronze sword on bronze shield,
Battles desperate fortunes,
And how, when age snows the hair
And the strength of limbs wanes?
Yet still stays the fire for deeds of high valour.
Better to go down to the shades,
Companions to the chieftain;
Than be slaves of some new invader
Or objects of contempt.

Sea Birds

Dazzling wind riders,
Balanced on the buoyant currents,
Sliding across the sky
With a flick of the wing.
To plane once more.
Aerial spies
On the harbour business.
A collective swoop
To dispose of choice offal.
Alight for a moment
On the chimney pots
For a session of hearty squawking.
Defiance maybe, or just
To jolly each other along.
Then in a wing flurry
Again to glide and slide
Above the green surf and spray
Fishing boats, and mere men.
In a superb air display
Masters of flight!

Spring Tide

The tide's in! The tide's in!
Excited voices cry,
And there it is!
Lapping with a foot of sand
To spare,
Just beyond the turf's edge,
By St Patrick's Chapel.
Wading birds paddling in it.
Dogs rushing up and down,
And a wonderful clean smell
Of seaweed and salt,
And above all,
Just right for bathing in!

Heather

Heather pours its purple
Over the hills;
Singing
'If you had summer
Luck was yours.
If you didn't
There will be others.
Soon, all too soon
The mountains will be touched
By first snows.
But we are here now!
Unique, wonderful.
Enjoy us, and be happy!'

Shambala

Autumn's heralds in the wood's blare.
Bright banners blazon forth
Gold, warm browns and scarlet,
As fires through the trees flare.

So may a rich foliage of idea and custom
In men and nations fall away,
Dance down to the ground.
Only the strong concepts and essentials stay;
Part now of a life that will shoot up
Vibrant in a different spring.

Now as the season changes
Sunlight pools in the still glades.
Time for reflection; selecting stores,
New journeys planned.
What should we take? What leave behind?
Soon, winter of the troubled streets,
And cold: no friend of the homeless.

After the snows, when the high passes open.
Our caravans shall go, over the windswept plateaus.
The great ice peaks towering;
Dazzling, all around.
Changing with each subtle shift of light.
Magical abodes of the gods.
They shall seek the far cities
And our lost brothers.

Angels

Angels of the way
Guard and protect us.
Give us deep healing,
That we may walk in our life paths,
With happiness.

May the children be blessed,
And talk to you,
And ask for your companionship.

May the readers of this book
Be blessed and touched by you.

When the time comes may you
Be there to help us;
In moving from this to that,
Without fear,
But with thankfulness.

October

Sunbeams lightly touch leaves and lie in pools.
Step out cheerfully about the day's doings!
Ride horses, gallop down the rides!
Dogs enthusiastically chase thrown sticks
Bounce around and eagerly wait for more -
Scuffle through brown crinkly carpets!
Snaffle elderberry fruit bowls!
Dodge the dropping chestnuts!
Admire the polished patterns of these wood gems,
A day to be alive in: walker's delight!
One for children to run about: revel in.
October's gift: for the heart's easing.

The Well

Clearer than crystal
Flawless!
The cool water wells.
Exquisite to drink
In the summer heat,
From stone arched
St Non's Well.
Mother of St David
In the Christian morning
Of West Wales.
Remembered the saint's last plea
'Brothers and sisters be joyful
And keep your faith'.
Royal blue the sea
Of St Bride's Bay.
Coloured cliffs
And fishermen cormorants.

Della McGowan

I am Della McGowan nee Coleman, I am forty-six years of age and I have been happily married to Ray for almost thirteen years, we have an eight-and-a-half-year-old daughter, Nikki who is a keen dancer with a very impressive 'trophy collection'. We live in Watford, Hertfordshire and have done for the past seven years, although I was born and bred in London. I come from a very close family and have one sister, Lyn. My father (Burt Coleman) is co-inventor of the Stylophone. I am sure you all remember Rolf Harris playing on one on his show in the late sixties!

Sadly I lost my mother during May '04 to a very short illness, she was seventy-five but didn't look a day over fifty even up until her final days. She was very special to me and a lot of my inspiration came to me around the time of her illness. I feel that my writing helped me with my grieving, and I have dedicated some of my poems to her in my book, which I am at the final stages of writing.

I have been writing poetry for many years now, after having been inspired by Pam Ayres. I have had several of my work published in various poetry magazines around the country alongside nine anthologies both at home and in the USA. I continue to submit my work as I am continuously writing new material. A lot of my work is aimed at women, and situations, some humorous and some serious. I enjoy writing humorous poetry and I find humour a very important part of life, although I drive my husband mad at times!

Apart from my writing, I enjoy music and I even learnt to play the drums (though not very well!) I also enjoy walking and keeping myself fit.

Must Be Summer!

You know when summer has arrived
The TV gets *more* boring
When starting up the barbecue
In minutes - it starts pouring!

The kids' long summer holidays
Which never seem to end
Those queues at all the theme parks
They drive you round the bend

Wimbledon and strawberries
The rain which *never* stops
Christmas cards and decorations
Selling in the shops!

Neighbours cleaning cars and windows
Weeding - mowing lawn
Doing all their DIY
Before the crack of dawn!

Overcrowded beaches
Loads of people - lots of queues
One sunny day on Brighton beach
Making 'front page news'!

Cards

I went into a shop to buy a birthday card
For my mate's twenty-third
They had a card for every damn occasion
Except that one, it's absurd

A get well card for cats, who've just been neutered
True, I tell you - I'm not joking
They even had a good luck card for someone
As they try to give up smoking!

Christmas cards in March! Congratulations cards
For passing an eye test
A multitude of cards, some quite amusing
Others too hard to digest!

I left the shop without my card I couldn't pick
A single one they'd shown
Instead, I went next door and bought some cardboard
Then I made one of my own!

Insomniac

Just lying there - can't get to sleep
Tried more than ten times counting sheep
Whatever I take, I just lie awake
Now my bed's up for sale 'going cheap!'

I tried self-hypnosis one day
Only once though, I just have to say
While relaxing both feet, I fell off my seat
As I got up my legs just gave way!

I'm not one to give up on trying
Though, I've spent sleepless nights awake crying
Over the years, I've shed that many tears
Could have filled up my bath - I'm not lying!

I've resorted to something quite drastic
Made a bed out of wood and elastic
When I climb in each night, I bounce up to my light
Then I knock myself out - it's fantastic!

The Doctors!

I called up my doctor this morning
To be honest, I didn't stand a chance
As appointments are 'out of the question' - (unless)
You book up five weeks 'in advance!'

I spent half the morning just trying to get through
After patiently waiting so long
When finally, a 'voice' on the phone at long last
But by then, I forgot what was wrong

Just as well, I was put back on 'hold', yet again
When my cat appeared, washing his rear
That jolted my memory, recalled what was wrong
And then everything seemed pretty clear!

The receptionist, she was just so impolite
As for manners - they weren't on her list
And patience, apart from the ones on her book
Well, I tell you, hers didn't exist!

I sat in the waiting room, bored out my mind
With a magazine ragged and torn
An incomplete crossword, the answers 'all wrong'
It was printed *before* I was born!

After an hour of just waiting my turn
When they finally then called out my name
And in less than a minute, I knew what he'd say
'It's a virus' - it's always the same!

Are We Nearly There?

Our bags are all packed, almost ready to go
And the kids are both sat in the car
They've been there since half six this morning
As we leave they ask, 'Will it be far?'

After driving for almost five minutes, or more
Both the kids moan for something to do
As we start up a game of I-Spy, to pass time
The youngest shouts - 'I need the loo!'

We pull over to park in a lay-by
As I hold him up 'over the side'
The traffic is now at a standstill
So embarrassed, he goes off to hide!

We continue again on our journey
Pass some fields on the way - god, that smell
When the eldest one opens his window and says
'Daddy, stop the car, I don't feel well!'

It's lucky I packed extra wet wipes
As I used up the whole of one box
But I couldn't do much with that T-shirt
And I had to dispose of his socks!

We'd driven around seven miles, there about
Not too bad, in just under two hours
Then the kids start complaining, they're hungry again
But that old snack bar's now selling flowers!

By now we are all so fed up and depressed
And the kids, they are really upset
But I'll swing for them both, if they ask me again
'Hey Daddy - *Are we nearly there yet?*'

It's *Not* Fair!

My next-door neighbour's got a brand new bike
It's just *not* fair
My daddy said, 'You *have* a bike,
Your sister's one, you share!'

He told me 'money doesn't grow on trees!'
And hey, do you know what?
He bought a brand new car for Mum
That *must* have cost a lot!

I only want a bike, and some new shoes
For my new dress
I'd settle for that doll's house
And besides, it costs *much* less!

My friend, she's got a stereo
And telly in her room
A mobile phone with 'built in camera'
Video and zoom

It's just not fair, I want one too
I can't, I'm not allowed
I never ask for anything
So my parents must be proud!

They say I'm not 'hard done by'
That I drive them to despair
And everything I want I get
Then told 'me' it's *not* fair!

Bear With Me!

I had to make a call
It seems I didn't have a choice
All I got was orders
From a pre-recorded voice

Listen as I tell you how
I spent my entire morning
Sitting with my phone stuck to my ear
Constantly yawning . . .

'Press one to speak to orders
Press two now to complain
Press three for just the hell of it
Press four to start again!'

'Press the hash key to repeat this
Or the star key to go back
Press 999 for symptoms of
A 'minor' heart attack!'

I listened to the options
And could not believe my ears
After keying number two in
A real voice just then appears

'Sorry to have kept you
Just bear with me!' - so I did
Then fifteen minutes later
I was put through to some kid

He didn't have a clue
And left me holding on for ages
Then he transferred me to someone else
In finances and wages!

Apologised and told me
There'd be someone with me soon
Then put me back on 'hold'
With the most 'nauseating' tune!

By now I'd had about enough
It was doing in my head
Besides, the place was just next door
And so I went there then instead!

I had to make a 'quick' call first . . .

Fifty!

You've just reached the grand age of fifty!
It's not really that bad you see
Another year near to your bus pass
Every Thursday your 'blue tint' is free

You buy panty liners at 'two for one pound'
They're a bargain you just can't resist
As you search for your keys - you try not to sneeze
Then you cough, as you try not to p.ss

Your eye sight's got worse than your hearing
But you won't wear your glasses at all
As you go to your garden you keep saying, 'pardon?'
Miss a step and walk into the wall.

You shop at the market each Friday
Then it's off to the Derby and Joan
Meet up with the girls in your 'twin set and pearls'
Have a fag, and a drink and a moan

It's getting quite late - it's nearly half eight
And way past your bedtime by now
As you get out your seat you can't feel your feet
Try to take a few steps - forget how?

You finally get home and you're knackered
Have a cocoa and one slice of bread
You slip on your bed socks and hair net
Drop your teeth in the glass by your bed!

You've been asleep only two hours
A hot flush wakes you up in a sweat
Your stick on the TV it's 'another repeat'
Have you seen it before? - You forget!

You rush to the lounge in your nightie
Can't remember what for - then go back
By the time you get back to your bedroom
You realise you wanted a snack

It's morning the birds are now singing
The mailman delivers your post
An 'Emerald Card' a voucher for lard,
And brochure with trips to the coast

You look in the mirror - to your shock and horror
You notice a bloody great bristle
When you pluck it away your teeth go astray
When you talk there's a very slight whistle

As you get in the bath - you just have to laugh
Everything seems so much lower
You swear you've got shorter
One foot less than your daughter
And whatever you do is much slower

I guess fifty's not really that bad
After all you can still have some fun
You're not really old - at least so I'm told
For a year 'til you reach *fifty-one!*

Spring

The season of sheer bliss and happiness will always bring
A beaming smile upon my face when soon approaching spring
A whole summer to look forward to, with longer days, much more to do
The trees dressed up in blossoms, birds returning, hear them sing

Newborn cattle all around the fields so full of life, astound
Butterflies, once caterpillars, field mice slain by nature's killers
Budding flowers, nasty weeds, always grow yet no one needs
Foxes rear their young inside their dens under the ground

The fragrance of cut grass so fresh, it takes your breath away
The dazzling sun and rain creates a rainbow of display
Puddles of rain mirroring, so picturesque this time, when spring
With summer 'round the corner come what may . . .

Time

It comes and goes, but never stays
The years, the months, the weeks and days
The ticking clock, its hourly 'chime'
Those hands that give away the time

The moments of anticipating
Looking forward, then just waiting
That time you've waited for so long
Is there for you - but then it's gone

Good memories fresh in your mind
And bad ones which you left behind
Cherished moments way back when
The times you'll never see again

Go on planning for another day
Wishing your whole life away
The future holds a mystery
Yet no one knows what that will be?

Emotions

A wide-eyed baby's smiling face
Unaware of life's rat race
So innocent, just so content
Those times, it seems, just came and went

A racing heart, a dreamy mind
With thoughts of love - so hard to find
Emotions flying high then low
The sad times which pass by so slow

Such happy times you wished would stray
When suddenly they're 'snatched' away
Sorrow, anger, desolation
Dreaded thoughts of deprivation

Reminiscing, deep in thought
The years went fast, they seemed too short
Once contemplating times ahead
Now living for each day instead . . .

Eyes

The eyes they see so much, they take in everything around
As they observe
The sight is such a fascinating sense, at times
You can't put into words

A newborn baby tries to understand, the vision
So hard to perceive
Then stores up all those images for years
Until one day he will retrieve

A childhood memory so vivid, yet it seems like
Only yesterday
The visions of the past are so secure inside his mind
Don't go away

SpotLight Poets

Ian McCrae

Well, here I still am - living alone in darkest Suffolk, working behind the bar at the Swan, drinking too much, writing too little, but now I've got the bus pass. Sixty years old and still writing about love and heartache, it's pathetic isn't it.

I'm now one of the founding members of 'The Mid Suffolk Writers' Circle'; do I hear a fanfare of trumpets or is it just the wind whistling between my knees?

By the time this gets published, I'll have been writing for about two years (I'm assuming here that it will get published). People ask me at times where the ideas come from but I'm scared to ask the question of myself in case they stop. If you find any typographical errors it'll be because I'm typing with my fingers crossed.

If you've bought a copy of the book, thank you very much. If you've borrowed it from someone, don't forget to give it back and if you've stolen it - you crook!

The Day I Almost Dined

Bill dragged me along to the party,
A cake full of fruits and nuts.
I was a brown ale in a case full of wine;
Bill told me to 'but him no buts.'

So I made up my mind to be miserable
As indigestion at a wake,
But I licked my lips in spite of myself
When I saw the ice on the cake.

Such a tasty sight titillated my appetite
Like an alfresco lunch in a bower,
For the look in her eyes would provoke a sigh
From the heart of a cauliflower.

She was sugar and spice, she was everything nice,
She was a supper of hot buttered toast
Eaten before a friendly coal fire
While the wind blew cold from the coast.

I swore I'd dine on her forever,
Make her my diet for life,
But a dark man arrived at eleven
And said, 'I've come for my wife.'

He was the waiter at closing hour,
Who cleared away my repast,
Leaving me with an empty platter
And the prospect of singular fast.

The Too Blue Blues

I'm going to put another CD on,
This one is much too blue;
Something with a bit more rhythm
That won't make me think of you.
I'm going to turn that dimmer switch
And let more light upon the scene,
Because I'm tired of seeing shadows
Haunt the places you have been.
I'm going to cap that whisky bottle,
I've had enough Tullamore Dew;
I'm going to wash the glass,
Get the pot and mash a brew.
I've sat here too long feeling lonely
Like a single, blue suede shoe,
And please forgive me, if you're watching,
But I've had enough of mourning too.

Too Late

Now the years are gliding swiftly by,
I think of things I've failed to appreciate:
The silence of a soundly sleeping child,
The noise of a strong and healthy one,
The sharpness of hunger that spiced the meal,
But most of all, yourself, my dear.

Speak Softly

Speak softly to me, darling,
That's what I long to hear.
No carping or complaining,
No doubting and no fear;
No haughtiness, disdaining,
No anger, sob or tear.

Speak softly to me, darling,
Bring comfort, please, not pain.
I want to hear of love so,
The sound of sweet refrain,
See the colours of the rainbow,
Sun shining through the rain.

Let there be no coldness, darling,
No love-destroying plaint;
Take affection's finest sable,
Love's warmest blushing paint
And on my blank soul, if you're able,
Draw the image of a saint.

Speak softly to me, darling,
Take me to that special land
Where your gentle words caress me,
As warm wavelets lap the sand.
Whisper softly, darling, to me
And hold me by the hand.

Post Nativity Blues

Another Christmas Day is over,
The family's gone away;
The fridge is full of turkey,
Half the cake still on its tray.

Take two Christmas presents,
From one pour out a nip,
Put the other in the CD deck,
Press play and take a sip.

It was nice to see the grandson
Unwrapping his new toys,
But in a way I'm glad he's gone,
You see, all that noise annoys.

My Life On The Line

They rush and they roar, they rock and they sway,
Clattering down the permanent way.
Where are they going?
Why don't they stay?
They wake me at night and disturb the day.
I don't get an hour of peace and quiet;
If I made half the noise it would cause a riot.
They make the ground shake,
They make my doors rattle;
It's like living your life
In an artillery battle.

Oh, for a home that's far away
From the permanent noise of the permanent way.

Maybe, Baby

Maybe, someday you'll be sorry
When you're freshly out of thrills;
You'll maybe wish you'd someone solid,
If just to help you pay the bills.
You'll, maybe, wish someone'd love you
Even when you're in a grump;
Maybe, baby, the sort of someone
That you used to call a chump.

It, maybe, sounds a bit unlikely
But stranger things sometimes occur,
It has been known on odd occasions
For reality to blur;
You'll, maybe, remember when I asked you
And wish you'd agreed to be my wife;
Maybe, you think that I'd still want you?
Maybe, baby - bet your life!

Long Ago On The Queen's Highway

Do you remember a long ago day
When we two were both painfully young,
A black leather jacket, a bright motorbike;
As we raced down the road, round my waist you clung,
And love ruled the Queen's highway?

Do you remember that hot summer day
When we stopped the bike in a lay-by,
Climbed up an embankment, sat down on the grass,
In the warmth of the sun the wind was a sigh,
And love ruled the Queen's highway?

Do you remember and, please can you say
Why no longer we care for each other?
All those bitter words, now just what were they for?
And the silences too? Why did we smother
Love that once ruled the Queen's highway?

Forever Gone

'Too late', chimes the clock on the tower,
'You've missed the appointed hour.'
'All gone,' booms the hollow knock,
'For good,' grates the rusted lock.
'Gone where?' ask the leafless trees,
'Who knows?' then murmurs the breeze.
'Neglected,' says the cobwebbed glass,
'For too long,' sighs the knee high grass.
The ivies peep in at the window,
But cling to the secrets they know.
Now speaks the lone magpie, in sorrow,
'Hold out no hope for the morrow -
Opportunity seldom returns
And the candle of life swiftly burns.'

Birth Of A Poem

Strands of unformed ideas
Float freely through my mind,
Tangling, strangling saner thoughts
Until my intellect is blind.
How might I control them?
Ha, am I such a clown?
Just formulate the floaters
And write the buggers down!

A Matter Of No Concern

(For Laura who visited Bulgaria with the Prince's Trust)

No one seems to love her,
No one hugs her like they should.
She's not forgiven if she's naughty
Or praised when she is good.

Little food, no education
And her bedroom could be airier.
But does it really matter?
She's just an orphan in Bulgaria.

Thought

'I think, therefore I am,' Descartes thought,
According to a book on philosophy I bought.
So I thought thoughts that are long and thoughts that are short,
I think I've been thinking far more than I ought.
I'll have to sit down with a small glass of port,
I've been thinking so much that I'm quite overwrought.
I'm beginning to think, when I bought that book I was caught,
If I don't think less and do more, I'll add up to nought.

Rock Until I Die

Do you see those toes tap-tapping,
Do you hear those fingers snapping.
As the people start to sway,
I can hear a rock band play.

Oh, strum, guitar, strum;
Drum, drummer, drum;
Go, rock band, go;
Blow, sax-man, blow;
Play, piano, play,
I wanna rock all day.

Well, I may be living in the past,
But I think rock 'n' roll's a blast.
When I hear that heavy beat,
I gotta be on my feet.

If the band plays that rocking rhythm
I've just gotta be there with 'em;
Dancing with a pretty girl,
Swinging her round in a whirl.

So, strum, guitar, strum;
Drum, drummer, drum;
Go, rock band, go;
Blow, sax-man, blow;
Play, piano, play,
I wanna rock all day.

Oh, strum, guitar, strum;
Drum, drummer, drum;
Go, rock band, go;
Blow, sax-man, blow;
Play, piano, play,
Until my dying day.

From The Artist's Notebook

Firstly paint the sky (cerulean),
Not one cloud to call it home;
Fading as it nears horizon
(Add a touch of flake and chrome).

Outlined sharply against the clear blue,
An eager chimney strives for light.
And with alizarin, cobalt, ochre
I can paint this in just right.

From here the ridgeline stretches outward,
Clutching at the gabled wall;
As it fights to hold the moss-encumbered,
Uneven, peg-tiled waterfall.

Pugnacious dormer windows jutting,
Sun reflecting from their glass.
Ornate carving on the bargeboards
To add a little bit of class.

Down, now, to the old oak timbers
(Here, burnt sienna gives the hue,
Light and shade can then be added
With alizarin and Prussian blue).

Animal Tragic

If I were an animal
A mouse I think I'd be,
With a coat made of chameleon skin
To blend in where I please.
Sharp little teeth to bite you
If you should corner me,
And a taste for Mouton Rothschild,
For washing down my cheese.

June Macfarlane

I am a 45-year-old woman living in the north east of England with my husband Sam. We have been together for almost 27 years and most have been happy ones. We have two sons; both now grown and looking after families of their own. Adam is 26 years old and a newly-wed. David is just 23 but is a good family man with two beautiful children; Ethan and Joshua who make me a very young but happy grandmother.

I began to write poetry and a little prose in 2003 during a time of hormone induced depression. I found that writing helped me unburden some of the thoughts, memories and feelings that I couldn't communicate otherwise. Once I began it seemed I had unblocked an endless dam of words and thoughts. I write now often, although the depression has cleared up mostly. I have a very diverse collection of work but tend to focus mostly on imagery and metaphors. I am and have always been a dreamer and find the most fascinating material in my daydreams. I love the sky, clouds and water and many of my poems centre around these subjects. Also because I have been blessed with a wonderful family and upbringing I have many views to share on love and relationships and this often shows in my poetry.

I have for the last 12 years been involved in the weight loss and health industry. I lecture on healthy eating and try to help people lose weight and feel good about themselves. I have jointly written and published a current healthy weight loss eating plan. I am a partner in a company called Changes which is now a national company with a website and hundreds of slimmers within its membership.

Currently I test my poetry on the one person who has inspired me most in my life; my mother Joyce. As a child she encouraged me to read with her enthusiasm for books and words. As I grew older I learned to appreciate the power and beauty of words and imagery and this, I believe has been the foundation of my poetry. My mother and I still exchange books and scour the local second-hand book stores for 'little gems'. We discuss them and the joy they give us, endlessly. Now whenever I need a valued opinion, I turn to her.

My Return

Today the sun returned to my sky,
in a long-forgotten splendour of light.
Presenting me once more, with time,
replacing lethargy with lustful fight.
The light had been stolen callously.
Darkness swallowed my spirit whole.
Endless night without stars or moon,
had gripped and held my very soul.

Time meant nothing but an eternal need,
to silently implode with my own misery.
Screaming inside, but to others it seemed;
I languished in a bland kind of apathy.

Then the sun returned to greet me today,
painting colours so bright it hurt my eyes.
Furnishing my world with time once again,
hope fluttered inside like lost butterflies.
Night shares its place once more with the day,
my spirit, once weary, embraces the light.
The embers of depression are dying away,
cooled by the wings of my soul in flight.

Let It Pour

Heavy raindrops fell from above,
star shadows darkening the ground.
Iridescent tears traced the pane,
like crystal drop lemmings - Hell bound.
Eerie yellow hues distorted the light,
sullen, as if threatening tantrum,
like a jealous maid green with envy.
Gathering darkness, it curtained the sun.
Liquid black ribbons threaded the gutters,
flushing plastic and paper to the grate.
Wrinkled wrappers floated like boats,
bobbing cheerily toward unknown fate.
I watched the downpour from a distance,
as the misery echoed through my veins.

Poettree

Wishing tree,
of poetry,
bearing fruit
endlessly.
Planted spring,
tiny sapling.
Watching buds,
happening.
Fat in June,
full of bloom.
Every leaf
rhymes a tune.
Watch in fall,
as gold on all,
gilds leaves,
large and small.
Muse on leaf.
Poetic mischief.
Settling wishes,
underneath.
Poetry, poetry,
oh my wishing tree,
granting wishes,
on leaves for me.

The Entity

A presence in my room,
beyond closed eyes.
I see nothing.
A palpable energy.
I don't hear a thing,
I feel you though.

If I open my eyes, I won't see you,
listen intently, I'll hear nothing.
Oh, but yes, I know you are here.
Nothing solid, nothing visual,
yet I know you -
feel you like my own heartbeat,
and I know you, oh, how I do!
A bare whisper of a presence;
you hover there,
kissing my mind
like a shadow kisses stone.
You are reaching for me,
telling me what?
Your face, a silhouette
upon my memory;
flickering, not quite tangible,
too elusive to hold,
yet, I almost grasp it.

Beside You

Walking beside you, even the rain is warmed in your love,
melting on my skin like soft dew, as if under your spell.
The coldest winter day spreads roses on my cheeks.
Feel my soul, its glow like a soft amber candle flame.
I shine and bloom in the purity of your own light.

With you beside me, past pain is erased,
as if it was never scratched upon my heart.
The darkness holds no fear of hurtful demons.
You have built a fortress of protection around me,
with the impenetrable strength of your love.

You enfold me blissfully within your care,
and I find shelter in each kiss, each tender look.
I have found in you, my contentment, peace and joy.
My heart settles safely within the home of your own,
sighing as it finds love eternal destination.

Let our heart's wings entwine and fly as one into our forever.

Apathy

Above the town she hangs like a grey rag;
pale and dismal as washed-out cotton.
Mood today like yesterday's flat lemonade;
still, tepid, empty of sparkle and fizz.

Apathetic sky; lifeless and weary heaven,
you shade the day with your indifference.
Alone you travel the long daylight hours,
with neither dance, nor sound from winds.

Indifferent sky, no colour on your palette.
A masterpiece of grim hopelessness you paint;
no bold strokes of energy glimmer on the sea,
canvas of gloom stretched out horizontally.

Above us all, her mood hovers over the day,
gathering no clouds, nor rain as her shift ends.
She sighs and willingly hands over her reign,
to the cool dark descent of her sister in the night.

Bluebell

She is one of a million delicate creatures.
Waltzing on a melody in the soft breeze.
A whim of sunshine briefly highlights,
the shimmering of her sapphire gown.
In a haze of blue beneath the woods,
In the shadow of her protectors.
If only she could sing a sweet lullaby,
her song would melt a million hearts.
Delicate flower of immeasurable beauty,
cherished within her sisterhood home,
deep in the heart of a hushed copse
where a passing rainbow cried blue.
Her wildness fools her admirers
for she sways like a brazen maiden,
head shaking in a show of liberty,
concealing her vulnerable spirit.
She bruises with slightest brush of hand,
her slim petals weep blue blood,
left alone in the wilderness she thrives,
but hold her and you bring her demise.

She Is Here

French lavender still lingers in the air,
announcing her presence as if she were there.
The room still warms with the essence of her,
a pot pourri of emotions ready to stir.

Her empty bed holds onto reflections,
wrapped in her aroma, tears and affections.
Her dreams once played across these pillows of down,
sweet dreams of dancing in her emerald gown.

The room, undisturbed, since the day of her death,
is filled with her being and the love of her breath.
She is the smile in the mirror, the waltz of the dust,
the shadow in the window, and the hair in the brush.

The very air whispers the sound of her laughter,
like an echo of her soul to remind us long after.
Intense love is tangible here in her now empty domain,
but we carry her within us - an eternal flame.

Oh, how I yearn for the circle of her arms,
for those gentle kisses, like healing balms.
There were so many words I wanted to say,
so many memories have been stolen away.

Faded Day

As the twilight creatures begin to stir,
sky in half-light turns sapphire blue.
A smoky taste of burning leaves in the air,
awakens a moment of mourning for summer nights.
Then a chilled, brittle breeze snaps those thoughts,
and brings a second's wanting of spring's new love.
Acute sensations are churned with the leaves,
freeing casual memories and yearnings as they turn.

Winter sparks a fresh new love song in my mind.
Sweet, soft rhythm of powdery snowfall emerge.
Dreams of firelight evening beckon,
warm, cosy embraces and glowing nights of love.
Tea lights flicker, sensitive to unseen draughts.
Images of heavy warm blankets of eider down.
Cuddles of affection on dark, lazy mornings,
long, warm kisses at the wakening of dawn.

As the light fades swapping sapphire for jet,
I can sympathise with the disappearing day.
As my yearnings evaporate with the light,
turning regretfully to more mundane matters,
I sigh as I often do, when it's time to go,
shrugging off inspired memories and yearnings.
The seasons stirring in vibrant hues,
leaves me satisfied, ready to face tomorrow.

Tangerine Lake

The sun peaks out over the lake,
rising surely to embrace the sky.
Reflections shimmer gold hues,
like dew on an indigo surface.

The ink of night is swallowed,
down to depths untouched by light.
Dappled blue swatches emerge,
mirroring warm, earthy tones.

Morning yawns, stretches her arms,
embraces the newness of life.
She strokes the world with freshness,
staining colour on the living grass.

Amber shots are a sight to behold,
pink's winking through sapphire blue.
Blinding platinum silver flashes,
imprint the beauty, making a memory.

The water glows in sweet tangerine,
and the breeze moves it like silk.
Across orange surface like liquid embers,
dreams dance with awakening hopes.

The lake, now dressed, is ready for the day;
cloaked in sky, garbed in earthiness.
Visible only to seekers of peace;
a painted lake on a canvas of day.

One Last Dance For Grace

Softly the notes began,
slowly, they evolved from silence.
Rising like heat haze in the sun.
Scent of lilacs drifted into the room,
like the trail left by a bridal bouquet.
Yet the room held no living soul.
As the melody rose, it filled the space,
haunting the room with its sweetness.
Taunting the spirits with its grace.
Then; as if drawn to the forgotten music,
dancing in through the windows,
The winds tore into the old music room.
Awakened by nature's breeze-driven dance,
a graceful iridescent figure appeared,
and for one brief moment she waltzed again.

Wrapped In Madness

Smell the mildew in the first sickening whiff of air,
breathe and hold it within your nostrils for reference.
Yes! The fetid familiar aroma comes with the dark curtain,
and as it slithers back into your consciousness, you retreat.

Scramble now, squeezing within the far corners of your being,
in search of the elusive hiding place, never yet discovered.
Curling, shuddering, repelling are as useless as leaded boots.
No escape from the panic that shaves great pieces from your mind.

You are breathless now as the heaviness descends upon you,
smothering your will - all beauty and worst of all, hope.
The curtain moulds itself stickily like tar around your heart,
and you lick the boots of the madness as it reigns once more.

Market Day Heat

A sticky-orange heat hung over the town;
heavy, claustrophobic, airless density.
A heat laden with tiny, weightless insects,
caught in a hot film of cloying intensity.

A distorting haze rose off melting tarmac
into suspended traffic fumes - a psychedelic trip.
A blend of food aromas wafted up from open stalls;
a perfume of spoiled fruit, doughnuts and traffic.

Dishevelled shoppers beaten into sluggish gaits
trailed overheated, irritable children and heavy loads.
Shiny, un-mopped faces peered out from slowing cars,
waiting - trapped expressions - on traffic clogged roads.

A quiet siesta mood reigned in the noon hour,
market traders lolled, disinterested, in old deckchairs.
A line of people queued, restlessly for ice cream,
cool thirst for quenching ice's kept them rooted there.

Relentless heat beat down a submissive race,
hot pavement burned their soles and heels.
The sun scorched flesh on unscreened faces while a cat lay cooling
in the shade of car wheels.

Mariana Zavati Gardner

Mariana Zavati Gardner was born in Bacau, Romania on 20th January 1952, the daughter of Artillery Colonel(r) Constantin Zavati, a chemistry teacher and Iulia Bucur Zavati, a pharmacist.

She studied at Vasile Alecsandri Boarding College for Girls and passed the Baccalauréat with distinction.

She specialised in languages at Alexandru Ioan Cuza University of Iasi and graduated as Master of Science in philology, double first class honours.

She did a postgraduate course in education at the University of Leeds and postgraduate courses at Goethe Institut Rosenheim and Ecole Normale Supérieure Auxerre.

She has been teaching English in Iasi and Bacau, Romania and Latin, French, German, Spanish and Italian in high schools in the counties of Essex and Norfolk in England.

She has published various poems in 30 anthologies, 8 volumes of poetry, articles on literacy criticism and book reviews.

She is a member of The American Romanian Academy of Arts and Science USA, LiterArt XXI The International Association of Romanian Writers and Artists USA, The National Geographic Society USA and an associate member of The Poetry Book Society UK.

These poems are about feelings of confusion and exclusion vis-à-vis the contemporary world. They express the intense struggle to follow one's principles in 'an intense material world', that is gradually replacing one's spiritual side. The poems are an exploration of the relationship between individual and society, the individual with the unheard voice.

Whispers

Whispers are lying hidden
They might be reigning
Over the scarecrow at times
Disguised in the garden
By the river
Where newts assemble to die
At the end of summer

I feel the whispers of the roots
Of the dying trees when trying to breathe . . .
I feel the snails feeding on some flowers . . .
It has not been a successful summer
For those people who do not fit in . . .
The day is about to surrender . . .
The season is almost over . . .

Someone is still searching for some prey
By the blind scarecrow in the garden . . .
Nothing is ever forgotten
Especially the chunks of dirt . . .
There is fresh mud at hand
For alien claws to scarify
Beware . . . the day is about to surrender

The Fruit Of Rumour

Shine has brought some wild roses into bloom
The night before tormented rain has wounded
Handsome petals . . . warrant to hollow death
And in my dreams embrace a shadow . . .
A silent soul described as an eternal youth
A messenger of promise to fare my fruitless love;
Oracles crave in the past as ruins . . . the Lord of Time
Advises and shares wisdom after the fruit of rumour
. . . I need to touch your ghost in love

Quick-Moving Sands

Deserted view of causeways and shores
Love reflected in high waters
Still storms my indifferent soul
Like an island subdued to the vanity
Of one's image repeated again and again
In the vanishing quick-moving sands
I know you've been there . . .
Footprints are fresh and my heart
Is disturbed by deep breaking sounds
Impatience cannot cure the longing
Feelings reverse and hours worship
Voyages on missing gales and waves

My Quiet Room

Locked in my quiet room I count the steps
Day by day, up and down, in my mind
Trees grow tall in front of my home
I cannot see the people in the road . . .

My Lent continues into summer . . .
Devour the flesh of flying dreams
Dust lies wounded along the causeway
Journeys to holy places of pilgrimage . . .

The dead cardinal searches a way to Heaven
A glimpse of the eternal *God* . . .
Somewhere he shared the joys of children
And then he went alone and humble . . .

I cannot see the people in the road . . .
Trees grow tall in front of my home
Day by day, up and down, in my mind
Locked in my quiet room I count the steps

Being Given Away

There is a far away island where people are dancing
Before being given away to heavens
The tunnel is narrow, deceiving and meddled . . .
The islanders are dancing on and on
While the golf player and the woman like man
Are having a meeting . . . she has forgotten to shave
Twice a day in the shadows of the water skiing boats

What I say has no colour or meaning
Of some possible happy beginnings
Sometimes I might detect the flavour
Of the dead end . . . of some very old things
Left unshaken, unwholesome by the wrong debtors
The Time Lord has made some incidental holes
Where birds of prey are building nests

I should collect dust from arrivals, from departures,
Where fate and Heaven embrace hasty directions

A Postcard

One carries weight in a postcard
Beyond the start of journeys;
Moving around a riot of sounds
Or weaving against the hours . . .

Angles of buildings
Landscape the shadows
In various shapes to match;
Rhythm of touch on letters
Sense the identity of tides

Alas . . . turned upside down
A future is designed to ignore
All movable mirrors that might
Reflect profane images
Of expecting creations

Steaming Spring

Steaming spring climbing up the mountain
Raging storm for a choir, wild and hollow
Fire in the mirror, liege by birth . . .
Olive trees break under the harvest
Embracing the first light and the voices
Planets lock the memory of the past
Lasting true love in my heart . . .

Brides and grooms are holding hands
Crossing early or late sunny circles;
Day and night bear gifts in the hearts . . .
Thirst for affection . . . daring embraces
In sight of two constellations . . .
Two lovers facing each other across
The Dome of the Sky for transient certainty;
The God of Duality mastering the Cosmos
. . . Resurrection mirroring the lovers' path

Renew That Joy

Search for the names and clean the silent stones
That lie ahead of time and feel the grief so deep . . .
When the flesh is hurting on the dusty path . . .
A lonely soul is sailing along the silent way . . .

The Queen of the Night has filled the lungs
With the day just passed and like a flutter of joy
Without a smile is sailing to renew the clocks
On the welded path of stones and grasses

Joy has been left by destined hours

An Orange Blossom

I was searching for a book to read this morning
And found an orange blossom . . . pressed words
Imprinted tender petals . . . silent lights
On mountains drowning in azures overseas

Colours of the absolute . . . measure of prayers
The rosary and the abundant scent balance time
And debate the destiny from within and the Spirit
'Notre Dame de la Gorge, aidez-moi, s'il vous plaît'

So many pilgrims have been walking to this chapel
In love along wild flowers . . . souls open in grief
Familiar hurt . . . rhythm of tolerating hearts
Dreams of peace in sleep . . . theorems of life

Depths

Prophesies from the depths of the sea
Oceans beyond tales and promising science
Turn old into new; forever the essence
Of our world is rediscovered while in soul
Nostradamus is gliding above the universe
Of his predictions juggling with the zephyr
And the eternal youth somewhere so gentle

Oceans beyond tales and promising science
Prophesies from the depths of the sea . . .

Shadows

Windows as eyes into eternity
Windows as ourselves into certainty
Issues for tortured souls . . .
Images as guides to confidence
Windows into immortal love
Shores and high tides touching hearts
Seldom haste surveying interchanges
Time sometimes wiping shadows
Windows as eyes into love . . .

On the glass mountain
. . . beyond the silence
piercing . . . but no sound
trekking alabaster breath
airy hands tied up
dried tears
gasping mouth
an empty call
the ritual of dedication
in fluid sleep and silver toys
designed for golden saltimbanques
dissolving feelings
from past into the present

Eyes

Words are like brushes . . . sometimes like spades . . .
Digging deep, into the sadness of lonely afternoons
You will always be young in my dreams, while I grow old
The smile of the lime trees . . . the fire massed in the sky . . .
I catch a glimpse of your eyes . . . I bring back the spirit
Of distant youth . . . rivers are drumming . . . remote hours
Return blossoms shaking by the whirling dreams
Waters are troubled . . . a boat carries thoughts
Of yesterday dreamers . . . clouds, vegetation and rivers are one . . .

Many Days

Joy is the fruit
Emerging seeds of happiness
Riders on rainbows

Ages devour each other
One understands only
When silences have settled

Ships transcend souls
Many days to rise
Journey to Heavens

Everlasting sleep . . .
The tree of life
No branches or leaves

Too Many Words

Find the names hidden by
Lift the stones which lie
Stare the Fear in the eye

A lonely moth is sailing
A touch of air is failing
As the Fearful are bailing

The Queen of the Night
Is dying far from sight
A silhouette has a kite

Some clocks hide a seal
Words decline at the Mill
Too many are by the Wheel

Gail Copley

 I was brought up in the north of England. We were a large family of eight in total and we were relatively poor.

I was about ten when my mum and dad split up, so did the family. I was fourteen when I met my future husband. I became pregnant at sixteen without realising. I lost my baby. I married the day after I was eighteen. I had my first child at nineteen. We lived quite a good lifestyle for the next few years. My husband worked hard and played hard. I went on to have two more children. Tragically one of my children was killed. I went on to have three more children - one set of twins. I then left my husband and moved down south to start a new life my with children. My marriage was a very traumatic one. I brought my children up well and they are all happily settled now.

I first wrote poetry in 1980. I was in hospital carrying my twins. I had lost a lot of friends and family due to my marriage. The only person that stuck by me was my youngest sister, and if these poems are published I would like to dedicate them to her.

My poems are all about emotions. I've never really spoke to anybody in detail about my marriage or what happened to me. It is the only way I could release my emotions and feelings through my poetry.

My sister who supported me, moved down south. Everything seems really good now. I am happier than I have ever been. I have got everything I ever wanted. A new husband, who I love dearly and three grandchildren. If my poems get published, I will call the title of my work 'Emotions Through One Woman's Life'. These express exactly what I've felt and went through.

What Is Life?

Life begins in the womb
It grows to a beautiful being
Beyond all your wildest dreams
It's born into the world
Into many untold things
You play, you eat and you learn
To know the things that go on all around
You become adult and learn the truth
The world is hard and incomplete
You give and take and learn to love
You please and ease through all the sorrows
But then there are all the tomorrows
People say life is what you make it
That is not true, you are what life makes you
The path is set when you are small
The pace is set as you grow tall
Then comes the time when you are grown
You leave the nest from where you were born
You begin to find that life is hard
You learn to love, you learn to cry
You learn to feel, you learn to try
You learn to give, you learn to take
But most of all you feel great
There's only one life as we know
So make the most of what you've got
With all the heartache and the pain
The happy times soon come again
For all the things that happen along life's path
We would not change things we have had
Always remember one little thing
If along the byways you think this is not true
Just think of all the people
That are worse off than you.

Motherhood

Is watching while they grow
Is smiling while they play
Is teaching them the words
You are longing to hear
Is making them happy through the years
Is watching them peacefully as they sleep
Is trying to meet their every needs
Is playing in the garden
Is rushing through the rain
Is slipping in the snow
Is laughing in the sun
The look of innocence on their faces
As they open gifts galore
The needing and the knowing
That they are always yours
Motherhood is a wonderful feeling
One shared by many.

Happiness

Is an emotion shared
The waking up to sunshine
When it's really raining
The walking alone, yet
Feeling you are with everyone
The being a part of everything
When you are not
Happiness is overpowering
And yet you want to capture it
And make it last forever
Happiness is an emotion
Shared by everyone
At one moment in life.

True Friends

True friends are
Those who are around when needed
Those who say sweet things
When you are down
Those who like to share
Your happiness when they are around
Those who make you smile
Instead of frown
Those who take your worries
Away with ease
If you have a friend in mind
Whose done all these things and more
Through the years
Then this is a true friend.

One's Desire

To my one desire
I love you
More each day
I cannot explain my feeling
For it is locked in my heart
And will not break free
Till I know you feel the same way
Then and only then
Will it explode into untold happiness.

To Jim, A Friend

Life is hard
True friends are few
People need people
Like me and you
If along life's byways
You meet the ups and downs
As well as you
Then you are giving life
What you want life to give you
If you find happiness and fulfilment too
Then may it stay forever true
'For all eternity'.

Loneliness

Loneliness is being
Alone all through the night
Having once known
What it's like to share one's life
The sadness of being alone
'Cannot be told, only known'
By those who live through it
Some people cannot bear loneliness
Some accept it for what it is
Some fight to overcome it
Loneliness is an isolation
Unknown unless lived through it.

Love Is

Love is a magical feeling
A fast beating of the heart
As one's love is mentioned
The fluttering of one's stomach
As the two are meeting
The sense of floating as
The two are kissing
The wonderful feeling
As they are caressing
Love is feeling and caring together
Giving and taking together
Being two, yet being one together
Being loved by one
Is the most magical feeling
One can ever experience.

My Love

My love is?

The touch of tenderness
The taste of happiness
The wanting to touch
The needing to hold
The smell of his body
The touch of his clothes
The feel of his heart beat
So close to mine
Hoping that someday
They will entwine

This is my love.

Love Is Priceless

Whether rich or poor
Love is the same
That's the one thing in life
You cannot buy
A person's heart
It's the one thing that's made
That cannot be parted
From your mind
You cannot lie if you're in love
Whether rich or poor
The feeling's the same
Not just a game
Love is priceless.

Caring

Caring comes naturally to a person like me
I care for people and hope
They care for me
I care what they say, I care what they think
I care what people do
I like to think people know I care
Caring is a simple thing
If people do not care back
It doesn't matter
Maybe in years to come
They'll look back on me
As a caring person
That's enough for me.

My Perfect Man

One who's loving
One who's caring
One who's sharing
All his love with me
One who holds me when I cry
One who kisses me goodnight
One who wakes me with a smile
One who feels it's all worthwhile
One who will see me
Through the bad times
One who will give me pleasure
Through the good times
One who will share his life with me
That's the perfect man for me.

Sorrow

Sorrow is a feeling
Known only to one's self
An inner most bitterness
One wishes to let out
The pain feels unbearable
To heart and mind
The people seem so unreal
Even though they are there
To say what they feel
Sorrow is a feeling
To one alone
The one who carries the burden
And to them alone.

A Female's Love

Love is the most precious feeling
It's being proud of the man you love
It's feeling for his ever needs
It's wanting his love forever around
It's wanting to watch
Whatever he does
It's needing to please him
Whenever one can
If one has loved
With these feelings in mind then one has loved
True to thine
Own love.

Hurt

People who hurt people
Along life's path
Do not fully understand
Even if they are bad
Life's too short
To hurt anyone vindictively
If you fully understand hurt
Then you would never hurt
A living soul meaningly

My Children

My children today have changed so much
From childhood to adults I am so proud
Like any mother is
Three grown women and two grown men
What they have achieved and how well they have done
The love they still give me
The space we give each other
Although the closeness is still there
For all of us to share
When needed we are always around
Their lives are happy and I hope content
They seem to cope very well
Letting go was very hard
You know that day will dawn
They won't be by your side
You will be left alone
You hope the love and guidance
Will stand them in good stead
That they will live their lives
Knowing you are always there
The love they have given back to me
Since they left home
Has made everything worthwhile
May I say to each of them
Thanks for the love and care you have shown
That you mean the world to me
Even though you are all now grown

Grandchildren

Grandchildren are special and full of love
We get all the pleasure and the good
The smiles, the laughter and all the joys
The first kiss and hug and being called Nan
You have more patience, you have more time
To enjoy their company when they are around
It's like getting a second chance
With all of the nice bits and none of the tasks
It feels great and you hope it lasts
Only it never does, the time goes so fast
They have to go home with Mum and Dad
So really enjoy them while you can
They are our grandchildren and we are their nans

Irene Clare Garner

I am a postman's daughter, educated in a mid-Cheshire grammar school. One English teacher was a great encouragement to me - I have even written a poem about Mrs Wookey. I gained English Language and English Literature at 'O Level' but did sciences for 'A Level'. I do have a deductive, analytical mind and these developed skills and instincts can be used both mechanically and intuitively to produce distinctive poetry. Even a science background can give quantities of material for writing with informed insight. I try to use all my background and experience to advantage.

I trained as a scientist working in labs on various disciplines. I gained a BA with the Open University where I did cover two Arts Units amongst the plethora of sciences. These were 'Systems and Resources' and 'The Early Roman Empire and the Rise of Christianity'. I was not a Christian then, or even immediately afterwards. Occasionally through the years I have written poems when inspired by events or in love.

Since retiring from science God has told me to 'sing'. I am the desolate woman of Isaiah 54. I have tried to 'increase my tent pegs' with the object of singing in various ways. Poetry is an excellent way to 'sing my song' to the world; and I am taking every opportunity. Being God's servant I am interested in truth, perspective, reality, along with the very personal including love, history, healing and creation in their broad and narrow senses.

My love for 'word' is real and I read and write with others at various venues in this city - Manchester. I go to both church and synagogue and gain inspiration also there. I now write a diary, always having wanted to but often found that I could not face the empty page.

All That I Know

All that I know,
Felt and experienced,
Is bound within me.

I want to sing it out.

A song for the future,
Syntax of the past,
Recent and ancient.

Available,

Perspective isn't truth,
Perspective is reality,
Reality is the sum of all experience.

I see at street level,
But from a high building;

I lift my eyes to the hills.

Sing For Joy Oh Barren One

Sing before you die,
Sing before you breath your last,
Life is but a hand's breadth.
Sing not only in final desperation,
Sing with perfect clarity,
Give beauty to your own unique, complete and perfect song.
Leave a legacy -
Before committing everything to the gaggle of decay.

Sing

In case of freedom, sing your own song.
In case of song, listen with care.
In case of care, love your neighbours.
In case of neighbours, all race, creed and colour.
In case of colour think complimentary.
In case of compliment say thank you.
In case of thank you, you have a friend.
In case of friends know who they are.
In case they are free, sing songs together.
In case of together, know freedom.
In case of freedom, sing your own song.

Was I Rash?

Dive in
And through the door
Is mental and physical torment.
Isolation
Ignorance of the masses.

Souls spending solitary days smoking
. . . Thick, smoky atmospheres.
No conversation
No capacity to relate.

Relating to a narrow and plastic coated mattress,
One small space is all that is your own.
Someone else's music, trespassing your space, offending your ears,
Assaulting and penetrating.
Piercing the soul, darkening the centre of being.

Yet existing is all that is left; when the system is offended by drugs -
Existing is all.

Exist and act on the necessary
Exist and do the essential
Exist and sit
Exist in silence
Exist and listen.

Listen to the silence of your mind
        of your soul
        of your spirit

And *soar* with it.

Think It Out

I don't think,
On anti-psychotics.
Blank
Clean
Gone the diarrhoea of psychoses,
A fresh white page
A newly primed canvas
No pollution here,
Not a mark.
Every idea, all notions
Clean and purified.
Fresh starts
New beginnings,
Bleached and cleansed.
Potential for pure perspectives
. . . Just wait!

Clarabella

(i - on a tape published in the 1990s of Beatles recordings that had not previously been published
ii - from 'She Loves You')

Paul McCartney wrote a song about me.
'Clarabella, Clarabella, Clarabella, Clarabella, Clarabella,' i
No other lyrics,
Repetitive on repetitiveness,
Obsession?
No - *'you think you've lost your love*
I saw her yesterday!' ii

It's me he's thinking of,
But thinks nothing
Knows nothing.

The girls at school who hitched to The Cavern,

Said
Clarabella, Clarabella,
The Beatles have written a song about you!
Clarabella!
I knew they were taking the mik.
C-L-A-R-E said I.
That's my name,
Just plain Clare.

Moment Of Love

And there was a moment
isolated in time,
All movement was owed to his music,
eternity seized my soul.

Then

All that is
was
and can be
dwelt in his small room.

Give Us More

In case of love
There is not enough of it.

The government
Cuts the services
To those in dire need.

In case of dire need
Those in it
Are the most damaged
The most rejected
These acquainted with loss.

In case of loss
We all know it
Experience grief
Accept bereavement
As part of life.

In case of life
It is to be lived
Not cocooned or settled
Experience the unexpected
Living free.

In case of freedom
We need to know it.
Given a stake
In a free society
Knowing love.

In case of love,
There is never enough of it.

Grandad

If my grandad were a tree, he would have been the Tree of Life;
With leaves that bring healing to every tribe and nation,
He would bring healing to all the nations, he visited in the early days
    of the twentieth century.
He loved Fiji and Venezuela, Chile, New Zealand and all the rest.
He wanted the best for them all,
But got 1914 and its carnage.

If my pampa were a drink, he would be a cure for all ills.
A potion made up of love, forgiveness, gentleness and peace;
    knowledge and all understanding.
He would pour it out on those in need of solace and comfort;
Give a blessing to the anxious and afflicted.
He died when I was seven.
I mourn him still.

If my grandfather were a fruit,
His seed would be both pip and stone, an infinite germ of life.
He would give abundance to the future,
A fresh and new beginning,
Life for life,
New life for new birth,
A garden, an orchard, a vast forest.

If my grandfather were a chair,
He would be the most comfortable chair in the world.
So he sat on the rocks at the topmost peaks of mountains;
Seeing a reality, a perspective, an horizon, a truth which stretches
    to the limit of experience.
He sat on the sandy beaches of Fiji,
Watching the Pacific Ocean in all its moods,
Whole and secure.
He knows the absolute now.

Mum, Dad And Grandad

I shall never see them again?
I don't believe that's true.
I will see my mum with Pampa -
Meet grandma Elizabeth
For the first time.

I will see my dad and
Meet Sarah Anne,
Know how she is with the
Real Jack Garner.

Percy Garner was quartermaster
Of the Eighth army,
In Italy 1944
Monte Casino,

'Butter, butter, 'scrapings of the gutter'

'Lard, lard, I scraped it off our yard'

'My eyes are dim, I cannot see, I have not brought my specks with me!'

In the quartermaster's store!

Shed Blood

After the battle,
The green fields are red with blood.
After the slaughter,
Streams of ferrous iron water the earth.
Leaving ancient reminders
Of events long past.

After the crucifixion,
The tree is drenched in blood.
Coursing down its veins and grain.
Leaving a scar -
A stained witness -
Of ancient miracles and decisions.

After 2,000 years,
We still fight -
Argue and debate - disagree;
Blood is still shed in conflict - war,
The innocent blood of children.
Not every innocent takes the blame.

Temptation - Golgotha - First Century Palestine

Was Yeshua, Messiah tempted to make crosses,
In His father's carpenters shop,
While cruel Romans ruled?
I think not -
Maybe he travelled the known world -
Walking the straight and easy roads,
Invaders roads
Open to everyone;
The world was getting to be a smaller place,
Twenty-one centuries ago.

So - who was at Golgotha
That day,
When the future of the whole world was decided?
Was decided? by God.
A future with Him at the centre.

There was - the child - the little girl who was raised from the dead.
Yeshua said, 'Talita kumi!'
And she was back with her mum and dad.
What had she seen?
What did she recall?
Who does she now look forward to?

Also the soldier with the nails,
A Roman minion maybe not even a centurion,
The lowest of the low;
He knocked the nails in -
Hammered the nails into his clean feet;
His healing hands.

His Healing Hands

Nor Mary nor John understood.
Mary needed her son, she was losing Him.
John did not know how much He loved Peter and the others.
Then John became Mary's son.
He took her into his home.
Greater gift no man leaves His friend,
A mother who was to become the 'Mary Mother of God'.

But - Mary Magdelene,
What of Mary?
She clung to Him, as she saw Him raised.
He touched her - and -
Seven demons had come from her.
She sat at His feet - listened, rapt.
Mary had anointed Him with costly nard;
Poured perfume on - his head - his feet.
Anointed Him with quantities of oil,
Wiped it with her tears, her hair.

She anointed Him as King,
King of the Jews,
King of the Kingdom of Heaven,
King of this Earth, all tribes and nations everywhere;
If only we accept His healing hands.

Spotlight Poets

Denise Hackett

My name is Denise Hackett. I am married, have 3 grown up children and I am 55 years old.

I have been writing poetry constantly for many years, and have won some small prizes too. I have had my poems published in over 50 anthologies and my work and photograph presented in the Poets Hall of Fame.

I had my first book of poetry published last year - 'Golden Verse'. My second book, which included a short story, 'Golden Heart', I wrote myself and it will be published later this year. My books are on sale in a stately home gift shop too. I sent a copy of my book to Belvoir Castle, and Duchess of Rutland wrote back to me with her personally signed letter. It stated how much she enjoyed my work, which I truly treasure.

I've worked very, very hard with my poetry over the years. It's been my heart's desire and dream to get published, and hopefully one day I will be successful too.

My poetry has had some publicity in newspapers, along with a live radio interview on local radio Trax FM - and one book has even gone as far as Australia.

I've written a poem about the famous Hannah Hauxwell and also received a prize for my work too.

I was brought up in Cantley Estate near Doncaster, coming from a large family of seven in total, I am the eldest.

Life's Ups And Downs

There's sometimes more downs than ups for me,
Like a glazier in the sapphire seas,
A stumbling block which stands there firm,
The tides of fortune sometimes turns -
Stormy waters, waves weald high,
Heavy heart, emotions run deep - sigh!

The tide will turn sweet days ahead,
Tranquil waters, compassionate words said,
Sunshine beaming down full force,
Like fields of sunflowers, pretty yellow gorse.

Fragrant meadows, starry skies,
The amour by day, and a night-time surprise -
Trees with blossoms sweet and pure,
Sunset lingering, life opens up the door.

Like pages in a book,
Sometimes painful to take a look,
The winds blow a new tomorrow fair,
Everglades, birdsong, nature's fruits to bare,
Waterfalls cleansing the fragrance and bloom,
June roses inspiring, perfume.

Glorious Sunset

At the end of the day the sun bows down,
All the time it has glowed like a crown,
A red sapphire shining in the skies,
Over the ocean, until sunrise.

A wonder of beauty so profound,
Roaming the clouds, then comes to ground,
A kaleidoscope of colour, then to dim,
Wondrous world we are within.
A tranquil sight, a burnished haze,
Lays the clouds to rest, till the sun does gaze.

Tried And Tested

They say things are sent to test us in life,
Ardent tasks, such trouble and strife,
Some are tested more than others I think,
I have someone else's share, my ship does sink.

Turbulent waters, you have to wade through,
Coming out the other side, good and true,
Simmering emotions, nerves jangled to the edge,
I hope to come out smiling, it is my solemn pledge.

Don't send me more grief right now,
I have a field of harvest, I now must simply plough,
Endurance test, brought to the limit,
Such catastrophes, well looks like I'm in it.

God gives out no more than you can handle at once,
But you feel so drained, there's a poor response,
Please let go of my heart strings so firm,
I don't want to squirm, along like a worm,
With pain in my heart,
Fire in my soul to depart,
Relinquish this turmoil, unwind me like a coil.

A Serene Dream

In my dreams I float serene,
Clouds of love, I reign supreme,
Mansions set in total grandeur galore,
Wondrous gardens, waterfalls, flowers demure,
I'm a regal lady, living so grand,
Life of sheer luxury, I'm in total command.

I ride out in my limousine,
Sit at garden parties, finest cuisine,
Latest fashions, I can wear each day,
In my dreams, to God I pray.
I have such a romance,
Love so divine,
Walking through vineyards, producing fine wines,
Grand attire, in sumptuous furniture refined,
Floating on clouds, from time to time.

Faraway Lands

I simply have the travel bug,
Going places supreme I dearly love,
Yearning to visit faraway places,
Home of culture, and many graces.

To sway among the palm trees,
Gently warming to the breeze,
To dance in my grass skirt around,
On charming islands, newly found.

The silken white sands, tranquil seas -
I long to linger and capture these,
Mingling amongst the natives there,
With orchids lay'n amongst my hair.

Dewdrop pearly sounds from steel bands,
Many thoughts of my promised lands,
Enchanting, cherished, dreams to savour,
The longing, enhancement's full flavour.

Victorians And Status

The Victorians with embellishment and status grand,
Super beings who once enriched our great land,
All the gentry, magnificently dressed,
Crinoline ladies there to impress.

Featured pin-ups wearing such style,
Victorian editors, with books to compile,
Flamboyant lifestyle so ornate,
An elegant lady sat to contemplate.

Voluptuous parties, and great balls,
Hold on to your partners as the night falls,
Ballrooms so lavish, gowns exquisite to the touch,
A charming era, that brought us so much.
Grandeur and pleasures to delight every eye,
Seaside trips, immense fun, no time to sigh.

The Power Of Love

This true emotion, conveying deeply a love potion,
The power felt from within creates such a desire,
A warming heart, a soul on fire.

It's so endearing, it's invigorating from within,
A feeling so immense, the light never dims.
You're a princess on a carousel ride,
True devotion felt from inside.

Hands entwined, our candlelit suppers,
Glints in your lover's eyes, golden cuppas -
Mingling in a dreamy haze,
A wanton beauty, a sunlight glaze.
The lantern burning deep into the night,
Moonbeams enhance all milky white.

To be together as one,
Lovingly surrenders, like in a song,
Sunkissed mornings, captures Cupid's arrow,
As dawn breaks, a sight of a sparrow.

Stately Homes

Stood with such grandeur, for all the world to see,
A splendid euphoria of treasures for you and me,
To savour over their beauty,
Encrusted with gold,
Regency striped wallpaper, regal and bold.

Endearing rooms, filled with elegance and taste,
Where all the gentry, sat for luncheon in true grace,
Portraits so gallant adorn all the walls,
Outside in the gardens, streams and a waterfall.

Raining In My Heart

As I walk down the country lane,
Raindrops patter from whence I came,
I picture love under my umbrella,
Buying a rose of love, from the street seller.

I try to stop the raindrops forming in my heart,
Trying to turn them to sunshine to never depart,
A symphony does play nearby,
As raindrops in my heart I cry.

People pass by as I walk along,
I try to capture your love in a song,
A cloud burst has just transpired,
But this is not what my heart desired.

Hearts, Cherubs, Roses

These are my lucky emblems,
I treasure most dear,
They were displayed on my wedding day with such cheer,
Roses in my bouquet, golden eucalyptus fayre,
Such an array of splendour measured with true care.

Those hearts adorn my necklace, with the cherubs too,
Golden was my veil, with teardrops to subdue,
Hearts, cherubs and roses, set upon my dress,
Glorious gaiety, so stunning such a bless.

The Summertime Garden

An exploration of fantasia - colour,
Some trees, and shrubs remain quite duller,
Roses open up their fragrant hearts,
The black cat emerges, and over he darts.

Those petite little petals formed of the shamrock,
Amazing how some flowers grow and interlock,
The ultimate lily stands supreme,
An ablazen of shades, such a gardener's dream.

Pansies with their pert little faces,
An abundance of delight, with many graces,
It's so spiritual in this garden dream,
Established with flowers, the best to be seen,
Glorious - oasis in your own backyard,
Green fingered culture, you've drawn the trump card.

Spotlight Poets Information

We hope you have enjoyed reading this book - and that you will continue to enjoy it in the coming years.

If you are interested in becoming a Spotlight Poet then drop us a line, or give us a call, and we'll send you a free information pack.

Alternatively if you would like to order further copies of this book or any of our other titles, then please give us a call or visit our website at www.forwardpress.co.uk

Spotlight Poets

Spotlight Poets Information
Remus House
Coltsfoot Drive
Peterborough
PE2 9JX

Telephone: 01733 898102

Email: spotlightpoets@forwardpress.co.uk